coding Games
in SCRATCH™

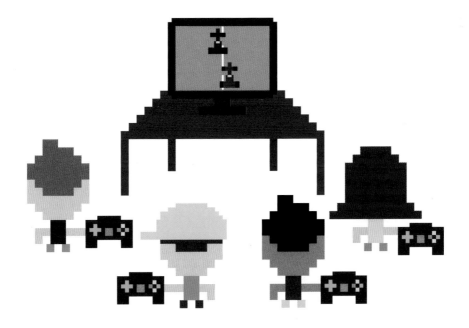

coding games
in SCRATCH™

JON WOODCOCK

DK UK

Senior editor Ben Morgan
Project editor Ben Ffrancon Davies
Project art editor Laura Brim
Editors Lizzie Davey, Ashwin Khurana, Steve Setford
Designers Mabel Chan, Peter Radcliffe, Steve Woosnam-Savage
Consultant editor Craig Steele
Jacket design development manager Sophia MTT
Jacket editor Emma Dawson
Jacket designer Surabhi Wadhwa
Producers, pre-production Jacqueline Street, Francesca Wardell
Senior producers Meskerem Berhane, Mary Slater
US editors Jennette ElNaggar, Lori Hand
Managing editors Lisa Gillespie, Paula Regan
Managing art editor Owen Peyton Jones
Publisher Andrew Macintyre
Associate publishing director Liz Wheeler
Art director Karen Self
Design directors Stuart Jackman, Phil Ormerod
Publishing director Jonathan Metcalf

DK INDIA

Senior editor Suefa Lee
Project editor Tina Jindal
Project art editors Sanjay Chauhan, Parul Gambhir
Editor Sonia Yooshing
Art editors Rabia Ahmad, Simar Dhamija, Upasana Sharma, Sonakshi Singh
Jacket designers Priyanka Bansal, Suhita Dharamjit
Jackets editorial coordinator Priyanka Sharma
Managing jackets editor Saloni Singh
DTP designers Jaypal Singh Chauhan, Rakesh Kumar
Senior DTP designers Harish Aggarwal, Vishal Bhatia
Senior managing editor Rohan Sinha
Managing art editor Sudakshina Basu
Pre-production manager Balwant Singh

This American Edition, 2019
First American Edition, 2016
Published in the United States by DK Publishing
1450 Broadway, Suite 801, New York, NY 10018

A catalog record for this book is available from the Library of Congress.
ISBN 978-1-4654-7733-0

DK books are available at special discounts when purchased in bulk for sales promotions, premiums, fund-raising, or
educational use. For details, contact: DK Publishing Special Markets, 1450 Broadway, Suite 801, New York, NY 10018
SpecialSales@dk.com

Printed and bound in China

A WORLD OF IDEAS:
SEE ALL THERE IS TO KNOW

www.dk.com

DR. JON WOODCOCK MA (OXON) has a degree in physics from the University of Oxford and a PhD in computational astrophysics from the University of London. He started coding at the age of eight and has programmed all kinds of computers, from single-chip microcontrollers to world-class supercomputers. His many projects include giant space simulations, research in high-tech companies, and intelligent robots made from junk. Jon has a passion for science and technology education, giving talks on space and running computer programming clubs in schools. He has worked on numerous science and technology books as a contributor and consultant, including DK's *Computer Coding for Kids* and *Computer Coding Made Easy*, and DK's series of coding workbooks.

CRAIG STEELE is a specialist in Computing Science education who helps people develop digital skills in a fun and creative environment. He is a founder of CoderDojo in Scotland, which runs free coding clubs for young people. Craig has run digital workshops with the Raspberry Pi Foundation, Glasgow Science Centre, Glasgow School of Art, BAFTA, and the BBC micro:bit project. Craig's first computer was a ZX Spectrum.

Contents

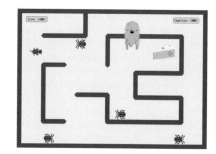

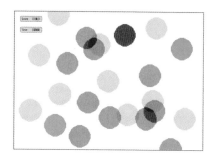

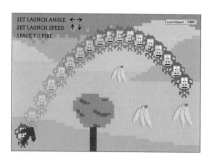

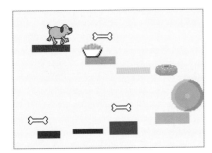

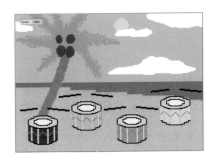

Find out more at:
www.dk.com/computercoding

Foreword

Many of the people who have shaped our digital world started out by coding games for fun. Bill Gates, cofounder of Microsoft, wrote his first computer program at the age of 13—a tic tac toe game. Just a few years later a teenage Steve Jobs and his friend Steve Wozniak, who later founded Apple together, created the arcade game Breakout.

They started coding simply because they enjoyed it. They had no idea how far it would take them or that the companies they were to build would change the world. You might be the next one like them. Coding doesn't have to become a career, but it's an amazing skill and can unlock exciting doors to your future. Or you might just want to play around with code for the fun of it.

Computer games open up worlds of imagination. They reach out across the internet and allow us to play together. They are packed with creativity, from music, stories, and art to ingenious coding. And we're hooked on them: so much so that the games industry is now worth more than the movie industry. It's huge.

And now, instead of being just a player, you can become a game maker too. You can take control of every aspect of those imaginary worlds: how they look, sound, and feel. You get to invent the stories, the heroes, the villains, and the landscapes.

But first you need to take control of your computer. To tell a computer what to do, you need to speak its language and become a programmer! Thanks to languages like Scratch, it's never been easier. Just follow the simple steps in this book to build each game and you'll see what goes on inside each one. Follow the chapters in order, and you'll pick up the essential skills you need to design and build your very own games.

Let's get coding!